CW00673094

Hermetics And The Aura

A. S. Raleigh

Kessinger Publishing's Rare Reprints

Thousands of Scarce and Hard-to-Find Books on These and other Subjects!

- Americana
- Ancient Mysteries
- Animals
- Anthropology
- Architecture
- Arts
- Astrology
- Bibliographies
- Biographies & Memoirs
- Body, Mind & Spirit
- Business & Investing
- Children & Young Adult
- Collectibles
- Comparative Religions
- Crafts & Hobbies
- Earth Sciences
- Education
- Ephemera
- Fiction
- Folklore
- Geography
- Health & Diet
- History
- Hobbies & Leisure
- Humor
- Illustrated Books
- Language & Culture
- Law
- Life Sciences
- Literature
- Medicine & Pharmacy
- Metaphysical
- Music
- Mystery & Crime
- Mythology
- Natural History
- Outdoor & Nature
- Philosophy
- Poetry
- Political Science
- Science
- Psychiatry & Psychology
- Reference
- Religion & Spiritualism
- Rhetoric
- Sacred Books
- Science Fiction
- Science & Technology
- Self-Help
- Social Sciences
- Symbolism
- Theatre & Drama
- Theology
- Travel & Explorations
- War & Military
- Women
- Yoga
- *Plus Much More!*

**We kindly invite you to view our catalog list at:
http://www.kessinger.net**

THIS ARTICLE WAS EXTRACTED FROM THE BOOK:

Hermetic Fundamentals Revealed

BY THIS AUTHOR:

A. S. Raleigh

ISBN 1564593703

READ MORE ABOUT THE BOOK AT OUR WEB SITE:

http://www.kessinger.net

KESSINGER
PUBLISHING

OR ORDER THE COMPLETE
BOOK FROM YOUR FAVORITE STORE

ISBN 1564593703

Because this article has been extracted from a parent book, it may have non-pertinent text at the beginning or end of it.

LESSON IV

THE AURA

"Aura" is from a Sanskrit word, which means literally "that which flows." It is something flowing out from a common center. Now, the aura in regard to man is really the etheric double, the astral body, together with the life-force, prana, and the mental body—and by the mental body, we include the causal body, the mental body in Theosophical literature used in reference to the lower manas; that part which is made up of the four lower notes, or sub-planes of the mental plane. The causal occupies the three higher notes of the mental octave; but in our usage of the term, we include the causal as the part of the mental body. The aura includes all that we have gone over. But that is not all. The aura also includes the soul, and the spirit, the Buddhi and the Atma. The six principles of man, excepting the gross physical body are included in the aura. It is the combination of the six principles which constitutes the aura. If we are to understand what this is, we must begin with, the etheric double, or magnetic body, which permeates every cell and tissue of the gross body and extends beyond it. We have, entirely permeating this magnetic body, the astral, or desire body, which passes through and permeates this and extends outward. There is, at the same time, permeating the astral body, the prana, or life force. Then, we have the mental body, which permeates this, and then, in turn, the causal body permeating the mental body, although ordinarily, we use these two together. The Buddhic permeates the causal body, and then the spirit, or

(31)

Atma, permeates the Buddhic body whenever it can.

Do not get the idea, that so many people have of stratifications. The idea that some of the epicureans used to have in Greece, that the different principles are in layers, one outside of another, (something like onion skins) is entirely erroneous. To illustrate, let us suppose that we have a box filled with marbles. The marbles will represent the gross body. There will be quite a number of cavities between them. In the same way, we now put in a lot of shot, and let that run in between the marbles. This shot will represent the astral body. Then we fill our box with water, letting the sand absorb the water. The water will represent the life principle. In this water there is air. The air, now, which is permeating the water, will represent the mental body. The oxygen in the air, which is permeating that; let it represent the causal body. Now, permeating this oxygen is the prana. The recognition of this fact, that the prana is separate from the oxygen, allows us to represent the Buddhic body. Now, the spirit will be represented by something as permeating the prana. This goes beyond the ordinary comprehension, so the illustration cannot be used any further here. But bear in mind, that one principle is permeating the other. It is not a lot of shells, one outside of the other.

The finer substances penetrate the grosser. Let us see what this implies: Remember, that the various principles have their different colors. And if you look at an aura and see it in its completeness, you will see the aura —you cannot see into the body—surrounding the body by an outflowing substance, a kind of aura flowing out which will be pink, or the color of a fresh-blown peach blossom. It will be sufficiently near that color for you to recognize it. This is the magnetic body, the etheric double. Then, you will see permeating this, flowing outward, a kind of aureal, so to speak, which is of the color of some shade of blue—it may be of different shades. If it is of any shade of blue, it is the astral body. At the same time permeating this, you will see a radiance of rose color flowing out and through all this, flowing all the while through it. This is the life principle, Prana. Permeating this astral you will also see a yellow glory, so to speak, which will represent the mental body. No matter what shade of yellow, so long as it does not approach orange. Then you will see an orange light, which is shining through and flowing out through the yellow; this is the Soul, or Buddhi; if you look still deeper, you will find shining out through all this a white radiance, the Atma, or the human spirit.

There will, also be seen a number of modifications of these fundamental colors, according to the perfection of the Aura. These are the colors, which the bodies assume, at least they will assume some modification of these colors, and when those colors have been assumed, then we will see the quality, the value of the aura.

If a person, or a patient, is sick, if he is diseased, morally or physically, you will see that the aura has a certain amount of dirt, so to speak, (that is the nearest way we can express it, the sensation which you will get) there will be a dirty appearance present in the aura. It will present the conception, or appearance, of being soiled, and whatever amount of dirt there may be in the aura it will be here indicated; either moral or physical pollutions. The clearer the color, the freer from contaminations. Clearness in a certain principle indicates its freedom from all contaminating influences. Then, brilliancy, the brightness which it assumes, indicates its degree of perfection along its own particular line.

Now, all these together form the aura—the outflowing,

which is flowing out from the center. Remember, the aura is generated within those principles, and represents those principles as flowing out. We ordinarily speak of them as being beyond the gross body. As a matter of fact, it permeates the entire body in our ordinary consciousness; we mean that body which extends beyond the gross physical body.

The aura is egg-shape, usually extending from the top of the head downward to the feet. The gross body is in the center of the aura, standing in that position. The aura extends on an average, from about two inches to two feet around in every direction from the gross body; although in the case of a Mahatma, the causal itself is about the size of an ordinary two-storied house; and in the case of a Buddhi, his aura extends for about two miles in every direction, and he is perfectly conscious of what is going on in that radius of space; different people, however, have it representing different states of being. Towards sunset, you can let a person stand at a distance from you and you will be able to see the aura, which he gives; you can see the etheric double radiating from the body; but for most people this is impossible. Then there are some people whose sight is so acute, that they can see in an aura a number of different bodies.

Now, do not get the idea, that the aura is confined to the human being. There is no greater error than assuming that the aura is peculiarly human, a human acquirement. The aura is found in animals just as much as it is in man, though they are not so perfectly developed. It is also found to vary according to the degree of perfection of the animal, and it is found that the principle is precisely the same as it is in man—the only difference between the aura of an animal and that of a man, being only in degree, not a difference in kind. This proves conclusively to the Occultist that the animal has the same seven principles just as man has. Man is in no way superior to the animal except in degree; the septenary principle is the same. For this fact, we are able to see animals clairvoyantly. The aural communication not only passes from man to animal, but from animal to man.

We used to have a friend in Arkansas, who raised numbers of sheep to sell and to kill for meat, etc. He told us on a number of occasions he had gone to the pen, and had made up his mind to kill a certain sheep; and immediately without the making of a motion, the very moment he had made up his mind in regard to the particular sheep he was to kill, that one would begin to make frantic efforts to get away. There was no trouble to find the others. But if we assume that the telepathic communication of man's thought goes to the consciousness of the animal, then we can understand these things; but not otherwise. Now, there is another peculiar thing; a wild animal is not afraid of a person who never kills animals; a vegetarian can get a great deal closer to a wild animal than a person who believes in eating the meat of animals. If you go into the matter thoroughly and clearly, you will come to the realization of the fact that the animals have the capacity for acquiring a knowledge of the intentions of the person toward them. Now in India, Yogis will go out into the Jungle and lie down and go to sleep, and while they are asleep the tigers will come and lick their bare feet. Anybody else would not dare to go there without an eight-bore rifle and two or three native attendants. They have nothing but love, and never eat meat, never take the life of an animal, and the tigers recognize them by their aura. They sense those conditions, that state of their being.

But it is not simply that animals possess auras, but

plants likewise. We have gone through an orchard and we can literally taste the peaches and apples growing on the trees. This is a statement of facts. We can stand ten feet from the trees and taste the fruit, and not even know how it tastes. Now, the only possible explanation for that, is that the aura of that fruit is radiating out and filling the air. Not only is that true, but you can put a plant or fruit in the room, set it down on the table and without touching the fruit at all, without knowing what kind it is, we can tell whether it is sweet or sour. We have seen women paring apples and have made the remark, without having tasted them at all, "My, how sour those apples are." That is clairgustea, in a sense, in some state of development. There must be a law underlying it. We see that every bit of fruit has its aura, not only a tree, but the fruit also. The odor of flowers shows that they have an aura; what you sense is the etheric double of that flower, its etheric principle. It proves the aura of the flower. But, this is not all.

Not only do flowers, plants, etc., have auras, but also minerals possess it. We know a lady down in Arkansas, who can take a piece of ore in her hand and by the taste, which she gets in her mouth, she will be able to tell you what it is—she assays it by the taste. Now, this proves in itself, that they have auras, else it would not be possible to tell them in that way. The sea stones, the looking into stones, the gazing into crystals, would only be possible upon the assumption, that they have auras, that they are souls, because their auras, their influence will establish there and become conscious of those things. But that is not all the evidence, that we have to offer. We have sat by the roadside, and watched the auric vibrations of rocks. We have watched them and seen the different colors emanating from them; we know that flint and rocks, just as diamonds, have auras, on a smaller scale, of course, not as perfect—they are there nevertheless.

This proves conclusively, that fruits, minerals, animals and wherever you turn have auras, and we are able to see these auras manifesting themselves. Remember, that it is universal throughout nature; there is absolutely nothing in the universe which is devoid of the aura; it is of universal application. It is the aura, or some part of it, which we see projected in the different parts of the air; they really are the doubles, and everything of that kind. You must bear in mind the aura contains the very essence, the very being of the being himself. No matter what the condition may be, it contains his mind, it contains also the very essence of his physical constitution. Consequently, if a person is sick his aura is diseased. It is not only diseased, but the specific disease, that he has, in a word, it has the spirit of that particular disease, and the great danger of infection is not in the bugs, bacteria, etc., it is in the aura, the spiritual emanation from the body of the sick person. The odor from the sick person is far more dangerous than all the germs in the world. The odor which comes from the sick person is really his aura. That is the thing, that we must avoid above everything else. A healthy person's aura contains the very spirit of health and good or bad, or whatever his character may be, is contained in it likewise.

But the aura of a man is electrical, that of a woman is magnetic; that sex principle is in operation throughout the aura; wherever you turn, you will see that it is in a state of constant operation, of constant manifestation. Now, falling in love, when it is genuine, is nothing in the world, but the polarizing, but the uniting of the masculine and the feminine, so the two polarize and become one. Affinity is simply when two auras, which are mutually positive and negative, unite. Divorce is when this affinity ceases to exist. The auras no longer polarize; thus they are separated. When a person becomes self-sufficient the aura is both positive and negative, therefore it does not require anything, but is self-sufficient—both the poles are found within. But in either case, remember the aura is sexed. Remember that the principles of the woman are magnetic and those of the man are electric.

Now, there is no greater piece of nonsense in the world than the talk some people have, that while the physical is electric, the astral is magnetic. That is all tomfoolery. The feminine spirit, causal, mental, body, life, physical and etheric double are all feminine. Those principles of the masculine are all masculine and so continue until we reach the point of sexual polarity within ouselves and both the sexes are developed, those principles have received their sex, and this fact may be recognized by a careful examination of the aura.

One who is able to study these things can verify for himself or herself, the truth of what we say. There is no truth in the opposite. The Aura is, therefore, the outflowing of the inner person of the being.

CPSIA information can be obtained
at www.ICGtesting.com
Printed in the USA
LVRC011452250820
664205LV00006B/29